Dévoiler

Kellen M. Parham

Kellen M. Parham

For more about the author and to find previously published books/poetry (i.e., *A Lover's Truce*, and more) please scan the QR code below:

Copyright © 2023 Why Not Publishing LLC

All rights reserved.

ISBN: 978-8-218-13680-2

Dévoiler

Dedication

To my cousin Scooby, college friend Moniquea Stanley, brother-in-law Ronald D. Pickering, Jr. (RDP), and Twitter friend Brittany Davis. Four lives who were beautiful and taken away far too soon. I miss my dogs. Y'all really got me writing writing. Thank you for blessing my life. I love and miss y'all like crazy!

Kellen M. Parham

Dévoiler

Table of Contents

Grief and Motivation — 5
On And On — 6
Sitting In Silence — 8
Scooby — 9
17 Years Ago — 10
Ghost — 11
Stay Black — 12
Don't Give Up — 13
Birdman — 14
Father To Grandson — 17
BIC Daddy — 19
Our Father — 21
Invisible But I Hope You Feel Me — 23

Life and Lessons — 24
Learning Lessons — 25
Faith & Greatness — 26
Imposter Syndrome — 27
Darkness — 28
Sunken Dreams — 29
Handling It — 30
On My Own — 31
HIPPA — 33
Let's Start Over, But As Friends — 34
Therapy — 35

Self-Acceptance — 36
Things I Said Yesterday, But Didn't Do — 37

Hypocrite	38
Imposter (No Syndrome)	39
Me For Me	41
Habitual Line Stepper	43
Love Is Awesome Really (L.I.A.R)	44
Argumentative Anxiety	45
I'M ANGRY	47
Making Amends	48
Family	50
Family	51
Motherly	52
My Father To Me	53
Gentle Tiger	54
Betty	55
Disciplined Child	57
Free	58
Dad, I Have A Secret	59
Help Me	60
Blackness Wrapped A Man	76
Black Love	77
In These Hands (God Is Blackness)	79
Black Like Me	80
Impure Bred	83
Wise Man	85
Knowing Then	86
Rhetorically Living	87
This Morning's Thoughts	88

My Garden	89
This Is Life	91
D.A.M. As Expected	94
The Crowd	96
In A Recession	97
Billionaires In Outer Space	98
A Martyr's Liberation	100
Don't Stop, Put Your Hands Up	101
Am I Next?	103
We're The Walking Dead	104
Acquitted Of All Charges	107
The Challenges	108
About The Author	110

Kellen M. Parham

Grief and Motivation

Death is inevitable
However, endings aren't always in vain
Pain fuels me – motivating
It's clear
I'm only here
Because of you

On And On

Haven't been the same
Since you've been gone
Waves of sadness
Drowning

Keeping my head above water
Getting harder
I'm tired

Mucky thoughts
Pounding
I'm mired

Don't know if I'll be able to move on
But I don't want to write
Another sad poem
Just want you back home

My open arms
May never close again
You were one in a million
My best friend

Wavering in this belief
I don't want to be
Alone
In this grief

Baby, please
I'm pleading
I'm needing
You

Please, baby
Tell me this is just a dream
What time are you coming home
Dinner is getting cold
Stop playing

Dévoiler

Come hold me
I'm getting cold
Too

These tears
Just won't stop flowing
And there I go
Floating

Sleeping
In a pond
From dusk
Through dawn

On and on
And on and on
And
Beyond

Kellen M. Parham

Sitting In Silence

In remembrance of RDP

Staring at a blank page
Trying to figure out what words to write
Listening for any trace of you
Sitting in silence, in the night

Today you were in my mind
In a space between a place and time
Reliving our memories
Endlessly in this heart of mine

Don't know what more to say
Towards a spot on the floor, I stare
Realizing it wasn't too long ago
You were standing there

The tears are swelling
But my eyes are strong
However, they can only hold back
The flood for so long

Don't know if I'm sitting in silence
Or if the silence is just sitting in me
Don't know if I'm sitting in darkness
All I know it's you, I cannot see

Dévoiler

Scooby

Where do the doves fly
After the funeral
When your favorite cousin dies

17 Years Ago

Every day I used to pray that I'll make it
Then my cousin gets killed
Then my homegirl gets killed

Every corner I'm turning around
I'm watching another body buried in the field

My prayers turned to asking God
Why the fuck are we even here
If we can die right before we've lived

Ghost

If you treat life as if you were a ghost
You could leap beyond the bounds of man
Defying all odds and obstacles at hand
And single-handedly stand
For an even higher cause

You could walk through walls
And walk across waters so deep
It'll seem as if
The depths of the abyss crumbles at your feet

You could walk through locked doors
Without a sight, without a sound
You'll have the power to influence everything around
You can alter a negative
Or build from the zero ground
To the highest elevation

With altitudes so profound
Beyond bounds
And the realms of the elite
You shall inherit nothing less
But the world at your feet

Stay Black

RDP's last words to me were, "Stay black!"

Don't sit around
Feeling depressed about me
I've lived my life in fullness
Parachute free

Feared no man
Followed my own beliefs
Took care of home
Left my heart
On the beat

Poured my soul
Into the wells of those
Needing me most
Lead a life I chose
Exceedingly so

So
Don't sit around
Feeling depressed about me
Get your ass up
Go for a jog

But most importantly

Stay black!

Don't Give Up

A loser is not, a man without
But a man within
Within a shell
That reeks and smells
Of rotten fruit and forgetful sin

In hell at heart
He's pale and dark
He sits alone
At home
Apart

From the world
He's hurled like an aimless dart
Hoping his target
Is not a brainless thought

A brand-new start
Indeed, he must
To leave a life
Conceived by lust

With each flick of his wrist
He heaves and thrust
One portion of wine
One portion of crust

He replenished his time
He deceived the dust
He couldn't believe
How he'd achieved so much
How he received Christ
In whom, he now believes and trusts

Indeed, he wasn't a loser
'Cause he didn't concede to such
Don't Give Up!

Birdman

I was born a bird
Born to fly
Born to soar
With wings kissing the heavens
As my mind explore

For what?
That, which I do not know
But one thing is for certain
Imma keep going
Until going can't no more

Underdog

Written for a friend

I am the underdog
One girl against the world
Back against the wall

I stand unyielding and tall
Head firm, held high
Facing the rambunctious streets
Watching life's adversities passing by

I, with high aspirations
To walk across this busy junction
My function of motivation
Is that I've walked too damn far
To quit now, time is wasting
Too much is at stake
To sit back and wait
But in the back of my mind, I know
It could take only one bad mistake
Leaving everything I've ever worked for
Extinct and erased

A clean plate
Left only with crumbs
Reminiscing on how they used to be –
A part of a whole
A part of a goal
A part of a bigger picture
But now a part of a story once told
A discouraging thought, indeed

I stand, both feet planted
Taking heed of the curb
Looking left, right, and back left
No longer afraid of the pain in sight
I just want to get what I deserve

Kellen M. Parham

People staring and glaring –
Her audacity, her nerve
How remarkably, she

Me
The underdog unafraid
And unacceptable to defeat
Relentlessly walking
'Cause soon enough I'll see
That every answer I've ever searched for
Was in my heart, within me; after all
After all, I am not the underdog
I am just who I want to be
And that is
Just me

Dévoiler

Father To Grandson

Battling complacency
And self-doubt
Deep inside this web
Of mine eyes

But this morning
I awakened with extra vigor
With the thoughts
Of Langston Hughes on my heart
Beating like a drum
Rompa pom pom

Don't you set down
  on the steps
  'cause you finds it's kinder hard

So today I vowed
To grab the bull by its horns
And take charge

As these are my dreams
Everything I've ever wished
I've come too far
Overcame too much
To lay down
And just quit

Unquestionably, my back aches
Legs sore, wobbly
To the point I can hardly stand

My focal point –
One foot in front of the other
Just to make it there
Is the plan
And I shall

Kellen M. Parham

The marathon doesn't stop
'Cause you have self-doubt

It continues
Bubbling bubbling
Bubbling bubbling
In life's baking pot
Smelling fresh as buttered biscuits
On a Sunday morning

So, grandson
Winning this battle
I know we're both yearning

But don't forget to
Keep on
Keepin' on
Keep on learnin'

And do as Langston
By getting up off them steps
But not 'cause we finds it's kinder hard
But 'cause today is our day
Today we reach new heights
Nestled amongst the stars

Ad Astra per Aspera

BIC Daddy

Jumped back in time
Paid my grandfather, Big Daddy, a visit

Haven't seen him since '95
They did a good job on the body
He used to call me Monkey Man
Even told me I was the Boss Man

He engraved that in wood
That plaque has lived with me
Ever since
Ever since
My first best friend
My momma's first prince
Gave it to me
As a Christmas gift

I miss Big
My cousins called him Big Daddy
But I called him BIC
Like the lighter
Because despite our
Struggles
He kept us warm
And he was dependable

Never indispensable
I'm still using your life lessons
And I'm 37
Long ways from that 10 year-old kid –
Right?

I miss you
My first best friend
My biggest big daddy
Remember back when
You took me golfing

Kellen M. Parham

And I used to be your caddy?

First and last time, I was called a nigger
I was in the golf course's swimming pool
10 year-old me, playing with another
Approximately, the same age, but white
I made sure to punch him in the side of his face
Hoping to shatter his brain
With all my might

Yet, you didn't find out
While you were there participating in the golf tournament
Making the crowd proud
I swear, you wouldn't have wanted it any other way

You taught me well
So, I taught that white boy too
All the lessons
Provided by you

Dévoiler

Our Father

I once met a Man
Who couldn't sit or stand
But could withstand
Any test at hand

He grinned
He bared
He got prepared
So scared, but not frightened
Fighting
He dared

His blood
His roar greeted the floor
Bones shattered
He's battered
While leaning for more
While pleading for more
More lashes, more gore
More slashes, the patches
His skin as it tore

More!
He said
As He stood past dead
Bring me your strongest!
Indeed that, they did
They beat at His head, His feet and His legs
Who knows defeat?
He repeatedly said

A rampant red
He repeatedly bled
While life continued to travel Him dead
Unconsciously, awake
For our sake and for our sin
His fate was a tragic death

So our lives could further extend
Amen

Dévoiler

Invisible But I Hope You Feel Me

Thank you for being here

Writing my life in invisible ink
Because I'm shy
And people are nosey
Judgmental
Comparing and contrasting
Declaring, hashtagging
For their own amusement

I write for my own edification
Not for your entertainment
Or your praise
Payments would be nice
But who in their right mind
Would buy a memoir
Of invisible words
Blank pages
Filled with
Love
Joy
Anger
Hope
Despair
And
Confusion
These blank pages are soothing

Staring
Imagining the words
Putting them into their perspective places
Filling in all the white spaces

So, here's my memoir
Continue reading on
The next pages…

Kellen M. Parham

Life and Lessons

There is this perception
That I'm not afraid of anything
But in reality
I'm terrified in every waking moment

Learning Lessons

There's something to learn from everyone
Big or small, from mighty to feeble
There's always a lesson to be learned
By a true believer

Faith & Greatness

Greatness starts
Within

The grain of
A mustard seed

Imposter Syndrome

A master
At my craft
An actor

I sit and I laugh
Though
There's a black hole
At the center
Of my soul
Consuming
All within my path

A master
At my craft
An actor

Everything
You plainly see
Fabricated
Sketches
Of make-belief

Entrenching the
Wearied
Rotten
Heart
Buried
Deep
Beneath

Darkness

Darkness, big brother
There's nothing more frightening
Than darkness, big brother

But what is rarely shown
Is often written in a poem

You want to know a man's truth
Tell him to pick up a pen
For his speech isn't thought provoking
Just a meager mechanism of defense

Sunken Dreams

Life is like an ocean bowl
Icebergs and storms
Sunk lots of dreams

What's buried deep beneath
We're treasuring
Sending submarines

Exploring all its wonder
Leaving us with more questions
To ponder

What more is hidden
Beyond the reeds
Beyond the shores
We plunder

Open yourself to the world, they say
Allow the light to show
But I don't think the light will reach
How deep I'm trying to go

But if fish can adapt
Then, maybe, so can I
Walk along the seafloor
No longer yearning for the sky

However long it shall take
I promise, I can manage
Alone, in the cold dark, searching
For my Titanic

My sunken dreams

Handling It

Only so long
You can lie to yourself
Only so long
Until you become someone else
Lesser

Wake up
Get the message
Stamp
Sign
Address it

Can you handle it
Can you handle
You handle
Handle
The
Pressure

On My Own

Taking my frustration
Out on these pages
But lately the rage, has
Been getting the best of me

Hopefully my family
Isn't getting less of me
Good lawd
Please
Keep blessing me

Addressing the
Pain
Which lingers
Dormant
Wishing it stayed asleep

It's this fear
That's keeping me, up
All night
Not happy until
I see morning's light

Almost slept through Christmas
Missed my kids opening gifts
Mentally drifted
To a faraway land
Of God knows where
Hoping it's peace there

I may never
Make it back home
Though I know
I'm not alone
As I roam
I have a bad habit
Of trying to handle

Kellen M. Parham

Everything on my own

Dévoiler

HIPPA

How long are you going to wait?
Until the sky swells?
Until the Earth quakes?
Until you're black & blue?

No, I told her tonight
How did it go
Terribly

Where will y'all go from here?
I have absolutely no clue
She's talking about therapy

Possibly, that'll work
I'm wishing y'all the best
Glad you were honest
You were – right?

Not a 100 percent
Expound
Oh, you didn't tell her
What you're doing
When she's not around

Why are you talking so loud?

Let's Start Over, But As Friends

If I can restart as your friend
Then hopefully
I can fall in love
With you all over again

I've done enough
For it to show
That my friendship
Was hardly onboard

This is my last accord
To make things right
I can't afford
To leave things quite
Not like
It's supposed, to be

We're supposed to be, deeply
Madly, in love
Unconquerable
Yet, here I stand defeated

Therapy

I am not ready
For these thoughts
To be real

No longer buried
Hidden deep
In the cold, dark
Inner chambers of my heart

Walking freely
Same as me
For the world to see

Why can't they just sleep
Rest, peacefully
But this time, maybe
In the warm, bright
Inner chambers of my mind

Still, out of sight, but
Much more comfortably

Not walking freely
Same as me
For the world to see

Is that not fair, enough
To not seek
Therapy

Kellen M. Parham

Self-Acceptance

*(originally written on a bar napkin
December 11, 2021)*

*Been a while
Since I wrote like this
Had hope like this
Wrote words on a napkin
Dropped quotes like this*

*Had to go to the bar
To find a bar
Of inspiration*

*Praying
We don't have any complications
Changing the situations*

*Saying it out loud
Delaying, manifestations
Dreaming of our glory years
What am I chasing?*

Dévoiler

Things I Said Yesterday, But Didn't Do

Man, I'm going to clean the bathroom today
Do you hear me bathroom?
I'm going to clean you today

Man, I'm going to clean the kitchen today
Do you hear me kitchen?
I'm going to clean you today

Man, I'm going to be productive today
Do you hear me productivity?
I'm going to be productive today

Man, I'm going to trust myself today
Do you hear me self?
I'm going to trust you today

Man, I'm definitely going to love my babe today
Do you hear me babe?
I'm definitely going to love you today

I can't stop now
I can't wait
So I won't

Hypocrite

I'm a walking
Talking
Contradiction

I'm human
By every
Definition

Dévoiler

Imposter (No Syndrome)

There's not enough room
In this heart of mine
Though I'm trying, I'm trying
To open my heart and mind

Can't seem to find
The perfect time
To answer your questions
Truthfully

Staring at you, youthfully
Childishly, dejected
Wildish
But perfected
Organized

Optimized
Knowing every angle
Every ploy
To use your heart
As a toy

Once you're comfortable
Your concerns, I discard
Damn, that's hard
Saying it aloud
No
I am
Not
Proud

But damn, I know how to perform
I'm an actor
A master
At my craft

I sit back and laugh

Kellen M. Parham

Fulfilled by my past and all I've done
I'm just an imposter
Without
The
Syndrome

Me For Me

Do you like me for me
Can't possibly be
Due to what you see

At least, I like to pretend
That I'm a bad bitch
But underneath
I'm just me
In sweatpants and Vans
'Cause it's cold outside, obviously

I used to wonder what people thought
When they saw the car I drove
Though I never put my heart in possessions
Too busy manifesting
A less harsh road

Material things
Have little meaning
To a man concerned about, literally, being
Alive

Awake
To see the face
Of his children sleep
Closed eyes

Do you like me for me
I can possibly see, why
I'm a handsome guy

Smart
Have a joke or two
Love to party
Buying drinks
Too many
A few

Gots to do
I gots to do
Better
Been saying that since forever

Want to say nothing changed
See, I'd be lying
I've been trying
Applying
Action

Doing well
Better
Seeing the growth
With much satisfaction

So, thus, I'm asking
You sure, you like me for me
The handsome me
Or the bad bitch
With whatever's hiding underneath

Or am I out of scope
Nope?

You like me for me
Yes?

I hope

Habitual Line Stepper

Crossing the line, again
There he goes, again
Crossing the line, once more
There he goes, once more

True enough
There he goes
There he goes

Can't he see the line
Is he blind
All he has to do
Is look down

Can't he hear us shouting
The line, the line
Is he deaf
All he has to do
Is read the sign

Maybe, he can't read
Hmmm
What more could it be
Can't see
Can't hear
Can't read
He is befuddling

But as expected
True enough
There he goes
There he goes
Crossing the line, again
And again and once more

Kellen M. Parham

Love Is Awesome Really (L.I.A.R)

Trying to figure out what I need in this life
Trying to figure out how to succeed in this life
Trying to figure out
How much I'm willing to bleed for this life

When it's my time
Stopped the clock on my shoulder
When I look back over
Will I say,
I'm leaving this right

Argumentative Anxiety

Just get to the point already!
How I feel in argumentative conversations

Anxiously waiting to get back to my own thoughts
But I'm still listening
My divided attention is simply distracted
By how your lips move when you speak
Your eyes looking in several directions
And when you're making a valid point
Your eyes pause
You blink softly
Before they meet mine

Time slows
My anxiety increases
Screaming
Just get to the point already!

I let out a deep sigh
My eyes roll
Retreating
Shifting my body weight with every tremble
I am now hiding inside

Envisioning
Fear as a dark cave of nothingness
With bright flashes of truth
Just get to the point already, please? I'm scared.

My outer man reassures me
Don't be scared, young child.
I'm here for you.
It's okay. Just listen.
It's okay. Just listen.
For the truth
 is the bright flashing light
 of a beacon
 notifying you that help is on the way.

Lost For Words

You are right
Absolutely
Right

About
Everything

All parts
Every inch

Every sentence
Sent

There's nothing more I can say

Dévoiler

I'M ANGRY

THAT'S THE POEM.

THE END

Making Amends

Had a talk with the past me
And guess what he said,
 We're back!

Fact is, that was the tail-end
 of the conversation.
We actually had a long talk.
No, actually, he did a monologue.

Verbatim,

Remember me?
Remember how you were ready to get rid of me?
Remember these red eyes?
Remember how you cast me to the side
 'cause you thought I'd distract you from math?

Guess, what?
I forgive you.
Without those decisions
 you wouldn't be where you are right now.
Look at your family.
Look at your daughters.
Look at your friends.
Look at your parents.
Look within.

We had the same life goals.
Yet, I wasn't as strong.
However, I still live
 'cause you kept moving on.

Your strength is immeasurable.
Beyond numbers I can comprehend.
You are a literal mathematician
 and I'm just a poet by pretend.

 'I love you like fuck,

Dévoiler

My nigga!'
That's what we'd normally say.
'I love you, broham!'
Damn, you really gentrified
 our thoughts.
Whatta day!

Big bro,
Thank you.
For your hard work.
Your many sacrifices.
My apologies
 for my several vices.

Despite it all,
I'm forever happy
 to call
 you my brother.

Kellen M. Parham

Family

Family

You are as tall
As a giant
In my eyes

I find comfort
In your shadow

Motherly

Who needed sunshine
When I had you
Who needed rain
When my nourishment
Came through your soil and roots

Your glistening, sweet
Vibrant petals
Needled inspiration through
The fabric of our worlds

You shaded me
From all Earthy perils
Which cooled me
From the dreary heat

All of you is in me
And I'm grateful
Till this day you remain faithful
Nothing more perfect
Nothing more motherly

My Father To Me

Remember you have people
Back home
Who loves you

Remember you have people
Back home
Who believes in you

Remember you have people
Back home
Missing and needing you

Remember you have
A home
With actual people
Who have actual faces
Smiling
Full of teeth
And a clatter of feet

Remember the life you live
And all its importance
Remember, son
That I love you
Be safe

Gentle Tiger

In every heart of a tiger is a child
And though he fearlessly wonders the wild
His heart is warm, it's tender and agile

Mighty he is in stature
And to adversity, a roaring beast
His embrace is undeniably strong
But comforting, soothing, to say the least

Others gaze in awe of his majestic physique
But when I look into the eyes of a tiger
It's my father, whom I see

Betty

My Dear Aunt Betty
Has the personality
Of confetti
Every day with her
Are like the joys of my favorite meal

Seeing that spaghetti rhymes
I can't stop thinking about calling her
My Dear Aunt Spaghetti
But don't tell her that
I don't think she'll be ready

As I was saying
My Dear Aunt Betty
Has an unforgettable personality
Full of joy, full of laughter
I can always point her out in a crowd
Even if I'm sitting in the rafters

Very unique, special
Very much needed
She's given me love
Way more love
It's impossible for me to repeat it

Looking back over my life
The years of Kelly Pooh
(what she always called me)
I'm laughing right now as I type this
I'm telling you

Loving you for you
Taught me the meaning
Of the word unconditional
You've taught several life lessons
While I was young
And impressionable

Kellen M. Parham

I'm grateful, appreciative of them all
Auntie I love you
And I'm so happy to call you
My Dear Aunt Betty Spaghetti

Disciplined Child

Wiped my tears
Bowed my head
Stood humbled
In my place

Are you gonna do it again?
Momma asked

Poked out my lip
Shook my head
No, ma'am.

And I still haven't
Done it
To this day

Free

Views from a father
Towering over his daughter
As her hands holds the sky
Sunrays, a twinkling eye
He lifts her
High

Higher than the blades of grass
Above the soaring trees
And they spin
Swirling in the wind
Like Dandelion seeds
Free

Dad, I Have A Secret

Hey dad!
I have a secret to tell you.
Sure baby, what is it?

She approached me
Then whispered in my ear
Shut up, dad!

Help Me

My 4-year-old daughter while hitting me
I'm gonna beat you like they did Jesus!

And we never watched
The Passion of the Christ again

Dévoiler

Getting My Youngest To Practice

Kailen! Where is your leotard?
I don't know.
Kailen it's upstairs in the hallway
On the floor.

I don't see it.

Kailen, you're downstairs.
Of course, you don't see it.
Go upstairs and look in the hallway
On the floor.

I don't see it
Kailen, I guess you're done doing gymnastics?
No!!
Well...
Okay, dad.

Sounds of tears echoes through the hallway

Kailen what's wrong?
I don't like this leotard.
Kailen we're going to be late.
Let's go!

Sounds of tears gets louder

What's wrong?
I don't like this leotard
and I can't find the one I want!
Okay, okay.
Let's go look for it.

5 different leotards lay on the hallway floor

Is this your leotard?
No, that's Sissie's!
Okay, here's one.

Alllllllright.
Reluctantly she puts it on

Now go use the potty so we can go.
We'll be late.
Yes, Daddy!

Knocks on bathroom door

Kailen, are you okay?
We have to go.
What are you doing?
I'm pulling up my underwear!

She opens the door

Kailen, I think your underwear is on backwards.
Stand up.
Know what?!
We don't have time.
Let's go!
Hurry up and wash your hands.
We're going to be late.

Jumping into the car

Put your seatbelt on as best as you can.
Are you okay?
Yes!

35 mph in a 30
65 mph in a 45
85 mph in a 65
Arrives at gymnastics

Sitting in the car alone after taking her inside

I hate being late
If my daughter is late for practice
She will get in trouble

Dévoiler

Don't want her to be in trouble
Because of me
Her dad
I know what it means to be in trouble in sports

2 hours past and gymnastics is over

Hey Kailen, how was practice?
Good!
That's great!

Gets home

Wife greets us

"Hey Buppie, how was practice?"
My wife asked Kailen.
Good!
"What's wrong with your underwear?
Why are they backwards?
Kellen! Why are her underwear backwards?"

My wife was staring at me bewildered

We were running late…

Shrugs

Me and Daddy

My daughter & I decided to have a writing session. She thought it was fun. She laughed and was focused. She really inspired me to just write and be present. This is a result of our time together.

The soft glow of the sun
Through your windowpane
Just a soft reminder
There's happiness
After so much rain
Hold close to the hope
That love may flow again

As the birds sing
And in the clouds, they dance
I pray they remind you of your father
Of us holding hands
See the joy you brought my life
Made life grand
I love you much more
More than you'll understand

Beautiful Like You

Written by daughter:
Kennedi Raye Parham (8 years old)

If I were you
I'd be beautiful like you
I'd jump to the stars
To make it better

When you left, I was sobbing
Because I had no more left of you
I was singing in the dark waiting for you

At Wayside School you were waiting to come to me
You were sad there, oh
You came to me

It made me mad you left
I'll never talk to you again
I'm beautiful like you, you know
Goodbye

Kellen M. Parham

My Absolute Loves

Sweetest thing I've ever endured –
My 5-year-old daughter
Taking my hand out of my pocket
Just to hold it

I love you and Sissie more than anything
More than any person
Love y'all more than I love my own life
I'm ready to lay down my life
For you two

What do you want to do?
Are you hungry?
Anything you want
Everything?
Dream bigger, baby girls

Daddy has the world
In his hands
You'll never go without
Even if it's my last
My last drop
I'll squeeze out more

You're wonderful!
You're beautiful!
You're gorgeous!
I pray to God I can afford this
Whatever you're asking for

God, look here
I know how you work
Without any type of understanding
But look here, bruh
Don't fuck with me about my girls
I'll pull up

They have a beautiful future

Dévoiler

They're special
Listen to me
You hear me?

Bless them
Care for them
Cherish them
Appreciate the art you've made
For a chance

Let the flowers bloom
Send the sunlight
As often as you can
That's okay
We'll make it work
It's more than enough
We're truly thankful
For all you've done

We all love you

Kellen M. Parham

Aye, Fuck Death!

Might die tomorrow
Might die today
So tired of writing
About him

Give me wealth
Give me health
That's all
Fuck him

Staying true
Doing more
For myself
Aye
Fuck you

Why are you even here?
You have nothing to say
Whose judgment
Is it
Today?

You're always around
But never invited
Nobody is excited
When you're out
How about
You don't

Stay home, please
This not what we need
But you don't listen
Take Trump
Take Blitzen
Take Saint Nicholas

I'm predicting this
It's his fault

Dévoiler

My daughters still believe
She's too old
Though he has a hold
Of her
And I don't know
If I like it

But seeing them excited
Brings me back
Full circle
To the devil

Wishing I could kill you
Beat you
Bury you
With the same shovel

On my level
Never
A renegade
Shedding blood
On this page
Fighting
Until my end of days

Kellen M. Parham

Kiss My Babies (For Me)

Should I come clean
I should
But this isn't the proper venue
This is something
That should
Only be between
Me and you

Not between strangers
And a book, or two
But here I am
What am I to do

Can't put the cat
Back, in its bag
Willing to risk
All I have
Giving it up
So it'll become
All I've ever had

Nah, that's not what I want
I want it all
To never
Not have happened

However, I didn't have a care
Life isn't fair
To the Godly
Oddly, not
Here I am
You celebrating me
As though, I'm all you got

Meanwhile, my soul rot
Festering
Pestering
My every indiscretion

Dévoiler

Your suggestion
That I'm a good man
Is laughable
I dreamt about this moment

I'm going to die soon
I know it
I dreamt it
I'm a poet
So it's supposed to be

Everybody that's close to me
Hold your tears
So many years
We were living happily

Even if you didn't
Notice me
I'm floating, G
Noticeably
And that's all that matters

Be happy
For me
I'm at peace
Kiss my babies
For me
Please

Losing Sleep

Only time I realize I'm alive
Is when we're grieving
When family members stop breathing

Too scared to go to sleep
Before kissing the cheek of my daughters
In case I don't wake up

They don't understand
How deep anxiety breaks us
Losing sleep
Praying to God to save us

I Love You

(Circa 2010)

Your smile is heaven in my eyes
Warm like a cloudless sky
And when I
dream it's under your stars of a million kisses
Art has nothing on your vision
You're beyond perfect for picture
At times I feel that I'm just a morsel
In the sweetness of your American pie
But you have a flavor to die for, to try for
To give all that I got
Just for my soul to be whole
And one day grow old and soar
With angelic wings into paradise for
Just for 60 seconds of your love
My gift isn't the day's present
But the days presence of your essence
Your heart has been God's evidence
Of His existence
I'm truly grateful for my blessing
Though I often neglect it
Falling asleep without prayer
However, right now, today I pray
That I truly deserve to be here, with you
I love you
I love you
I love
You

6 Beating Hearts

What are you supposed to do
When you're done playing games
When you don't see life the same
Do you restart

What if what was once in your heart
Change
Where do you go
Who do you call on
Who does the punishment fall on
Who's to blame

Is it fair to blame myself
Someone else
On how we're living

If I'm not giving
All I have left
What's the point
How I'm any help

Feels like theft
All I do is take
Ransomware

Who truly pays the cost
Everybody
All of us
6 beating hearts
Lost

Fly Away Young Butterfly

Fly away young butterfly
There's not a drop of nectar
On these palms

Just calluses and rough skin
Paper cuts suffered from back when
Black pen wrote my plight in poems

Kellen M. Parham

Blackness Wrapped
A Man

Black Love

written circa 2006

Tangled within a web of mad confusion
Of a Black lover's illusion
Unknowing of whom to love or whom to trust
Just knowing of whom we lust
Black love, thrust into our hearts, by the fiery darts
Of Cupid's weapons of mass destruction

Bio-Terrorizing
The capitals of our red, white, and blue hearts with its Black dust
One sniff and a sneeze, brought the Black society to its knees
Black love rapidly spreading through our blood, and lungs
Like an incurable disease

And then we kiss our brothers and he die
And then we kiss our mothers and she cry
And then we kiss our sisters and she gets pregnant at twelve
And then we would have kissed our fathers, but hell
He was never even around, since the beginning
Guess, he was the one that kissed us

Fathers kissed his sons, and fathers had to run
So sons and brothers grabbed a gun, and began to run the streets
While mothers worked twelve to twelve, just to make ends meet
While twelve-year-old sisters in project stairwells, get freaked

And Cupid is still standing over the pot
Bubbling a block of Black love
He cooks it, chop it, stack it, pack it, and ship it
Making sure there is not any hood, urban, suburban
That doesn't get it
Gotta give Cupid mad props because the boy is gifted
The boy is so gifted, that he even writes songs about it

Whether its gospel, rap, jazz, heavy metal, soul, or hip-hop
Because every CD, sounds like Black love to me
Cupid even marketed his own way onto TV

Establishing his own channel
Of Black love Entertainment Television

Thus, creating multi-cultural generations of Black love
Thus, creating multi-discolorations of Black love
Different places, different faces
But still the same traces of Black love
And this is all just plain to see,
Just open your eyes when you walk down the street
Or better yet just turn on the news
"50-bullet barrage killed an unarmed groom"
Sean Bell was Black, in love like me
However, you may love Black love
But Black love ain't loving me
And that's Black Love

Dévoiler

In These Hands (God Is Blackness)

If I held the whole Earth in these hands
And promised to keep it safe –
Would you still shoot me dead in the streets
'Cause there's blackness in your space?

If I wore the infinite galaxies around my neck
Consisting of all sparkling specks –
Would you still rob me of all life
And leave me hanging in distress?

If I've sworn to you
With one hand held on my Book of Truth –
Would you still not believe
In all of these miracles you see?

Are my words alone
Not enough proof?

That I am human too

Kellen M. Parham

Black Like Me

What else Imma be
But black
Through-and-through
Outside
And internally

Wouldn't want it any other way
To be black like me
Through-and-through
Outside
For eternity

Don't be confused
By all you see
I wasn't born via grief
But through-and-through love
Via belief

My parents
Both black
Through-and-through
Outside
In matrimony
Kissed one night
And chose to have me
Wouldn't have been
The only me
But my sibling wasn't as lucky
To be born
Through-and-through
Black like me

So who do I owe this to –
Living through-and-through
Black like me?

Dévoiler

Is it to God?
Is it to luck?
Is it to my own strength?
Someone or something is responsible
For my existence
Don't know if they'd want to meet
'Cause I have questions

Are you even Black?
Do you even know what Blackness feels like?
Do you even know the struggle?
The pain?
The intensity?
The shame?
That I felt looking at my reflection

Have you ever felt rejection?
Not the one
Where it was due
To you
Outgrowing your clothes
And your momma couldn't sew
So you wore
What you woe

But the rejection
Of just being
Of just breathing
Of just blinking
Of just
Standing
On the corner
People watching
'Cause it's a beautiful day
In May

Why are there guns pressed to my face?
I don't sell weed
I don't even smoke
I'm literally standing here

Kellen M. Parham

On this corner
'Cause this is where I can best see
My skinfolk

Who are
Black like me
Through-and-through
Internally
For eternity

Dévoiler

Impure Bred

written circa 2006

We are bred, we are born
And we are torn
From our mother's heart
Fathered by phantasm
Through our mother's dark

Blinded, as I'm corrupted
I could see no evil
Though it seldomly
Whispered in my ear

Constantly plaguing my insight
Masterminding my fear
Still the scents linger
From everyone, who has ever been near
But I can't grasp, nor ask any questions
Because the truth, is never clear

So, who am I to you?
Am I: man or dog?
Do I have four hind legs, or do I have two?
See, I often forget
And the shit seems so inexplicable to you

Her words are so predictable, times two
That every man she has met
Are all selfish, liars and cheaters
She said, *He doesn't want us, but he really knows he needs us.*

Nine months passed, still ain't taking care of his fetus
All these condemnations, got me praying,
"Lord Jesus!"

Who the fuck am I, to turn these pessimists into believers?
Tied down, mind boggled

By their allegations and how they treat us
Dumbfounded and astounded, by their misconceptions
And bewildered by their weapons, used to defeat us

Indictment, deemed guilty, before innocence
Their verbosities of construed reality they feed us
So we're immaturely born, deformed, and feet less
Running with what they say as truth
Coerced to parturition my reality
Birthed through a black woman's youth

So I kneel at my pew
For my bloodline isn't of purebred
But that of an infidel male
And of a woman with a righteous creed
So I'm constantly drawn back to that question, indeed

Am I: man or dog?
Do I have four hind legs, or do I have two?
But actually, I wouldn't be a man
If I left that answer up to you

Wise Man

written circa 2006

A wise man sits upon his stoop
Old and drunk
Blind, deaf, and mute
Nonchalant, he piss and poot
While enjoying a cigar
Filled of his favorite toot

Ongoers shout
Unhinged and about
But he just sits
Chewing the cigar in his mouth

No smile, no frown
Not a blink, not a sound
Only the utter tapping
Of his cane on the ground

As he sits, he stares
Oblivious to what's being said
Just observant of their lips and body signals
From their feet to their heads
And all he knows is all he sees
A community of the blackest darkness
Who aren't as happy as he

Knowing Then

Arrogantly youthful
 I am, who I am –
  and you are?

The old wise man then responds
 At the wrong place.
 At the wrong time.

Solemnly
The old wise man turned away
Vanishing within the mirror

Dévoiler

Rhetorically Living

What hides behind the realm of words?
Is it everything you've ever seen?
Is it everything you've ever heard?
Is it everything you've ever dreamed?
Or is it just you – in a void that's obscured?

What is it that humbly drives us
 to what awaits us
 that's just not here?
Some may call it faith, where as
Others may call it fear

If it could be seen prior
 or even experienced before
 would everything that is read as good
 suddenly be no more?
And would this realm of words, utterly, cease to exist?
Or just continue on in chaos
 as we live disowning our only true gift?

Kellen M. Parham

This Morning's Thoughts

What's keeping us all from committing
Suicide, homicide, genocide
And from falling deep into that underside – the dark side?

The cynical, the pinnacle – destruction
Corruption, the abruption, an ending full of pain
What's keeping us all from going clinically insane?

Is it love, is it fear, is it God, is it clear
Or is that angel on our shoulder
Overpowering that devil in our ear?
Grandma always said that the end is near
However, many believe our worst days are in our rear

What can make a man who has worked hard lose his heart?
But what can make a man born beneath a world beat those odds?
Tell me, who got the answers?
And where were they before our aunties died from cancer?

What's keeping that dread in our mind
From becoming our master?
Where's that person that can bring us solutions, the answers?

28% of black single moms are living below poverty
But what kept that black family from falling into those statistics?
Was it smarts, were they gifted,
Or were their lives already scripted?
Is it really that hard or was it really that easy?

So, why is it that millions fail and fall
But only thousands are uplifted?
In society we've witnessed, our lives bleeding, our eyes bleeding
Their lies bleeding through these gauzes covering our wounds
So tell me – what's really keeping us
From being thrown off our rocker?
From being swallowed whole and consumed?

My Garden

Hello!
My name is Rose
And this is my garden
Not your ordinary garden
No vibrant colors
Or whimsical fragrances

Sounds of honey bees
Aren't whizzing amongst our leaves
Only bullets from the gang war
That was planted
Before me

Death's
Ghastly tree
Bearing fresh fruit
In the moonlight
Rotting
Choking by smoke
Of the humid jungle breeze

The gardeners
Routinely
Pluck the weeds
Most of them
Were my friends
Now gone
So here I stand
With a few others
But mostly
Alone

Onlookers approaching
Staring in awe
Sniffing their noses
For years I lived knowing I was different
But didn't know how so

Until I heard one say
Pointing in my direction
Mommy! Look at the roses.

This Is Life

written in 2002 at the age of 18

I sit and I write
This can't be life
It must be a dream
Well, so it seem
From the illusions it brings
From the schemes and plots
From not knowing where friendship begins
Or to where it stops

From crooked cops killing my brothers
With a motto, "To protect and to serve"
I've seen my cousin's blood
Chalked, outlined on the curb
From racial profiling
And urban neighborhoods neglected
Politicians, policemen, and drug lords
I wondered – if they were all connected

Project killings and murders
Without a killer to be found
From dope boyz in the trap
To boyz N da hood,
Smoking purp by the pound

A gravel life without concrete
To death we stay falling
Questions and problems
Like AIDS or cancer we're not solving
The doctor is calling
But health insurance we barely can afford
So we pray even harder
So our health can be restored

Families torn apart
By no father, or father with no heart

Neglect and abuse of their seeds
So I ask, "When will life start?"
This can't be life
This must be fiction
Poor kids and families
Thanksgiving wishing
No love, no home, no food
No Christmas; just wishes
Only left to dream
Of a big home with satellite dishes

Penitentiaries, death row
Death by lethal injections
Murder, suicides
Diseases and lethal infections
Nuclear weapons, bioterrorism, assassinations
The world's natural resources wasting

The fight to restore peace and equality
Shows no dedication
Hate, distrust, jealousy, envy
Community love feels so empty
Fiends murder for fifty
Not dollars, but cents
Just the walk to school and back
Is full of suspense
Residents filled with adultery
Teen pregnancies, and sexual assaults
Raping of minors committed by adults

Ignorance, bigotry
A Civil Rights Movement
Taken as just History
A memory, now plaguing my residents
Some had thoughts of black presidents
And no need for affirmative action

Yeah...

Now that's life, that's satisfaction

Dévoiler

But until then
I must deal with what's happening
Because this is real, this is life
But behind all the misery and strife
There is a higher power
Who shall make it right
See, you can't always change the world around you
Just yourself
Because this is Life

Kellen M. Parham

D.A.M. As Expected

Two people shot
One killed
In the parking lot
Of one of my favorite spots

As unfortunate as it might be
The news didn't shock me

The feel goods
Of the real hoods
Usually ends in tragedy
And in some places, nightly

A river of blood
Flowing down the street
Of my neighborhood's candy lady
Reminded me

Of a drug deal gone wrong
Walking from school
Passing the bullet riddled homes
The sounds of the 4th of July
Came early that year

Neighbors stopped to stare
At the display
Of a yellow raincoat
Painted red
Where the body used to lay

Swirls of red, white, and blue
Sparkled the night sky
Fear from the bombs bursting in air
Lingered on their faces
All that remained
From a clamorous celebration

Dévoiler

This sparked a new year for me
My life changed
From that moment, I knew

Life wasn't infinite
And when dues is due
Nothing is stopping
The soul collector
From coming through

Turkey D.A.M.
One of my favorite spots
Deadly
Fun
But as expected

The Crowd

In remembrance of Scooby

The crowd
I'm always in the crowd
You were once in the crowd
But no one in the crowd cries for you today

In A Recession

Faithfully
I walk into the valley of unemployment
With my resumes and applications
Along with 50 thousand other people
Sent on permanent vacation

I've ran so hard, during the job chasing
That my feet ache, burning
I think the devil took the souls of my shoes

The more interviews, the more bad news
Budget cutbacks
Another 5 thousand added to the job pool

This can't be life
Why does it have to be so crude?

Kellen M. Parham

Billionaires In Outer Space

The interstellar race
Of billionaires in outer space
I question
Is this really a competition
To reach Mars
Or simply, a means to escape

Who are they running from
Little poor us
Taxes
Disgrace
Ending world hunger –
Just to cause it
In some other place

They put a whitey on the moon
Back in Gil Scott-Heron's day
Meanwhile, his doctor bill
Just like us
He couldn't afford to pay

The price of food was going up
I mean, we all gotta eat
Living in rat infested
Low income, public housing
I mean, we all gotta sleep

A rat bit his sister
Her face and arm swelled
I wonder, if his sister Nell
Ever got well

This was 1970
3 years later
The concept behind the EpiPen
Was designed by none-other-than, who
The same ol' folks
Who put that whitey on the moon

Dévoiler

So now, my questions for you:

How many sisters died
To put that whitey on the moon
Or those billionaires in outer space

How many sisters starved
To put that whitey on the moon
Or those billionaires in outer space

And when that roof
Over their heads
And over ours
Scurried with rats

Did the whitey on the moon
Or the billionaires in outer space
Ever to Earth
Stop, look back
With questions of their own

On whether
Gil, his sister, and us
Having no doctor
No food
Nor shelter
Deserved that
To fend all alone

A Martyr's Liberation

ATTENTION BROTHERS!

What's the reason for our troubles?
Is it because our founding forefathers killed & raped our mothers
 then banished us to plow & harvest the infertile lands of
illegitimacy?

Tell me what happened to Father Time's civility?
Where are his caring hands and his passion to bring stability
 to a barren, arid land plagued by egocentricity?
Am I wrong or am I just lacking humility?

How can we smile & reconcile with our transgressors
 after continuous years of tears
Generational genocide, and exile?
No longer can we afford to waddle
Enslaved by their balls & chains!

WE MUST REVOLT!

We must become revolutionaries of change!
We must fight to restore –
Neither ignore nor make excuses nor cast blame!
We must allow love to bore its way back into our hearts!
We must depart from our vain ambitions
And become model citizens for our sons
With hopes to break these bonds of oppression.
Now is the time, dear countrymen.

NOW IS THE TIME TO DIE!

Dévoiler

Don't Stop, Put Your Hands Up

May God bless the family of Dillon Taylor

Hispanic man was killed
'Cause he couldn't hear
Died dancing to the vibes
Of his favorite tune

Out the door
Of a convenience store
He two-stepped, he spun
Eyes closed
Down the barrel of a gun

Last sound he heard
Were the sounds
Of the drum

Woke up
At a concert
In the
Kingdom

Don't
Stop
Put your hands up
The DJ, hyping the crowd

His body moved, grooved
To the smooth rhythm
Of the gun

Stage lights
Blazed bright
Again, he spun

Don't
Stop
Put your hands up
The DJ, even louder

Smoke flowing
From the stage
Smelling of gunpowder

Earphones in his ear
The DJ screaming, even louder
Don't! Stop! Put your hands up!

Am I Next?

Rest in Paradise – Roosevelt Brockington Jr.

Songs of peace echoes
In the killing fields
Young Black men
All dying in various communities alike

Just the other day
A black man was stabbed to death
In a hospital boiler room
While his good friend
Was on the other end of the phone

His poor mother pleaded
On the news from her home
Pleaded for the killer to turn themselves in

Tears swelled from my tv screen
Pain looked me eye-to-eye
It got me to thinking
Am I next?

Kellen M. Parham

We're The Walking Dead

What do you do
When the drugs and alcohol
Stops doing their job
Of numbing the pain

Life, being in your favor
How odd are those odds
To receive a standing ovation
A round of applause
For being human

Their lies bleeding
Through our gauze
Woven by the fabrics
Of our lives

But the difference between
Us and them
Is that we can feel the pain
I'm in anguish now
Typing this

Meanwhile
Texas is taking this book
Off of the shelf
Of the public library
'Cause I used the word cracka

Matter of fact
Lets add more words
To make them
Uncomfortable

Honky
Pro-abortion
Legalize marijuana
Gay marriage
Transgender rights

Dévoiler

Equality

Marriage
Between man and man
Woman and woman
Homosexuals adopting children

Vaccinations work
Thanks Dr. Fauci
MAGA hats lurking in the dark
A stark contrast
Between night and day

What more to say
If we die today
Who will carry the torch
But first make way for
Tiki torches and khaki pants
'Cause Black Lives Mattered

Dreams shattered
'Cause we didn't expect to die this soon
Thought I'd at least make it
To being a groom

Scary what a day could make
Less than 24 hours
Didn't have a chance to change draws
I died sour
Big Momma wouldn't be proud

But that's the life
Of a black man
Killed by a hand-me-down Klansman
In 2022

Plenty of hands applauded
My predator
My overseer wanna-be
Younger than me

White boy, from outta state
Carrying an AR-15
Over his shoulder
Scared like a sick puppy

So he say
As he walked
Towards the protester's way
Handing out judgment day stickers

Like
pop* *pop* *pop* *pop
Back up
Stop
Get back
pop* *pop* *pop* *pop

Acquitted Of All Charges

(God bless the families of Joseph Rosenbaum, Anthony Huber, and Gaige Grosskreutz)

Acquitted of all charges

Due to global warming
The killing fields are thawing
Past blood slushing on my boots
Skeletons grabbing at my ankles
Pleading for my help

Still fighting for justice
My ancestors haven't slept
400 plus years
Yet they cheer for us

You're doing great, son
Everything I wish I'd hear
But it's clear
I thought I was oppressed
Until I got dressed
And said
Fuck this shit

God gave me my breath
Not you
I'm going to be okay

Kellen M. Parham

The Challenges

Each poem represents at least one of my many day-to-day challenges. This poem is a reminder to just take a break and relax. Trouble don't last always. Enjoy your day!

Put your pen down
Pick your smile up
Flip that frown up
Switch your style up

The pain may pile up
But you possess the power
To devour
All obstacles
Impeding your desires

Plant the seeds now
Let the tears shower
And when the sun comes
Blooms the flowers

A thousand hours
Of chasing your dreams
Worth a lifetime
Trust me
You shall see
Dreams come true
Watch the outcome

I know it's challenging
But what is life
Without some

Dévoiler

About The Author

Kellen M. Parham wa born in Atlanta, GA, but partially raised in Lil Brooklyn, New Iberia, LA. He learned to harness the gift of writing while studying Mathematics at The Georgia Southern University (#GATA). Mathematics and statistics pay his bills, but it's through poetry where he finds purpose and freedom. Getting lost into his deepest thoughts is all he ever desires. Being honest and documenting those thoughts may end up being his downfall, but it's a risk he's willing to take. Embrace every thought you have he suggests – the good, the bad, & the unacceptable. Stop fighting them. Come to a truce. This is his truce. His coming to peace. No matter the cost. He loves his family, and he loves [YOU].

www.ingramcontent.com/pod-product-compliance
Lightning Source LLC
Chambersburg PA
CBHW060333050426
42449CB00011B/2748